C000115189

My Book For You, Friend

Hana Ibberson

Nehemiah 9.3 Mission
Word Confession Worship

Copyright © 2021 Dr. Hana Ibberson
Copyright © 2021 Deborah Ibberson for the illustration
Copyright © 2021 Bible Verses To Go for the image on the book
cover (https://bibleversestogo.com/)

ISBN: 978-1-3999-0223-6

All rights reserved.
For permission or inquiry please email: nehemiah9.3@hotmail.com

First Printing, 2021

*To spiritual seekers who are searching
for the answer of the ultimate question*

CONTENTS

PROLOGUE

It was a thrilling and heartfelt moment! I was walking with the divinity, *El* in His peaceful and glamorous garden as usual. It was not an ordinary moment but a special one. He sternly yet gently asked me whether I would like to do a unique mission for His Kingdom in a place called 'Earth.' I was much aware of His beloved planet Earth, so was quite intrigued by His errand. 'My Lord, what is the mission then?' I queried. He slowly started to talk while strolling. 'There are humanity down there who are lost and cannot find the Way to come back here,' He continued, 'sadly, they are the ones who once willingly volunteered to go down there to lead humanity to the Way up to here, yet have now totally lost their significant missions as well.' 'What happened to them while carrying on their missions?' I quietly muttered to myself but was loud enough to His ears. He steadily said, 'The cunning enemies as known as slaves of *Ha Satan* with various nicknames of *destroyers, murders, rebels, haters, betrayers, muggers, liars, deceivers, accusers, adversaries, abusers and rapers* are down there. They continuously and ceaselessly delude humanity in order to complete their ultimate mission - destroying My image bearers and then dragging them into the kingdom of Darkness- with the sophisticated tactics of temptations, luxury, pleasures, lusts, trials, doubts, deception,

1

dullness, depression, suppression, subjection, disobedience, rudeness, despair, hopelessness, life's worries and selfish ambitions.' I quickly noticed at that moment that His countenance looked saddened. A solemn silence! 'If I'm right, you're asking me whether I would go down there and lead them to the Way, aren't You?' I broke such heavy silence. 'Yes, if you can,' He continued, 'with one condition you can go down there.' 'What is it, my Lord?' He gracefully turned around and then sparklingly looked at me and said, 'I will wipe out all your memories we have had together here and then send you there as a vulnerable baby. You will be in a dark and secret place for 10 months before arriving at your destination. Sadly, many were unable to get to their destination because the enemy used his life-long successful tactic of abortion. Nevertheless, my faithful and courageous ones arrived there safely and are doing their missions as opposed to the ones who are lost. Rejoice! Many of my sons and daughters whom you call them here as *Heroes of Heaven* once went there and came back successfully after their honourable missions were completed on Earth.' 'That's good to hear at least, my Lord,' I said. 'Will you go, My love?,' He beseeched. 'If it is Your pleasing and perfect will,' I said after a solemn pause, 'then I will.' Bam!

One

Our Father In Heaven

What was that? Have I been lost in a daydream? Well, it was something that I cannot describe exactly. It is just like a 'wind,' you cannot see it but can feel it, therefore it exists. So was my daydreaming experience. It was something beyond my understanding. Would you argue that it means nothing because I cannot explain it to you properly? Who knows that it was something that you have been looking for, and even it is your life-long longing perhaps? As you continue to come along with me, you would know what it is in the end. Fingers crossed!

***

Friend, (hope that you won't be bothered by me calling you like this) can I please ask you a question (if you don't mind) although you don't need to tell me your answer now? 'What is a word that comes to your mind first when you would hear a word, "Father" or "Dad"?' Have you got one? Then, I'd like to ask you another one, 'What caused the word to come to your mind first?' I reckon that your thought process has just activated and is ready to roll, hasn't it?

The word, Father or Dad is so much more than just a title of a male parent of a child. It contains a *relationship* between two human beings. Relationship is literately defined as things are connected or one thing effects on another. Thus, I speculate that your first word came out of 'how you have connected with your father and what relationship you have had with him so far.' It heavily reflects on your experiences with him either positively or negatively in time past. Do you agree? I hope that you are not the ones whom I am going to talk about as below.

***

Sadly but honestly, I met several people who had terrible experiences with their fathers because they were traumatised or badly influenced by him. To them, 'Father' is a word on their wish list to cross out if possible. I have found that they were also struggling to connect with Father in Heaven because of their earthly father's image. Whether you admit it or not, you have inherited half of your DNA from your parents: 50 percent from your mother through an egg, and 50 percent from your father through a sperm. Actually, someone says that women do inherit 50 percent of their DNA from each parent whereas men inherit about 51 percent from their mother and 49 percent from their father. Anyway the half of you is more likely or just like your father whether you like it or not. Let's pause for a moment here and take a breath and then put yourself in your father's shoes honestly. What do you see? What thoughts come to your mind now? Have you ever thought that he also is a son of a father (your grandfather)? He also has the half of his father's DNA. So did your grandfather. We can go on and on up to the very first human being, 'Adam' meaning 'the ground' or 'earth' in Hebrew. Please bear with me even if I use some foreign words because they hold significant meanings in their languages. Did you know the reason why we all go back to the ground when the days of our life are ended? We were from the ground so that we go back to the ground when we finish our life. It's good to know about it, isn't it? Perhaps it helps you shift your mindset if you are obsessively focusing on the physical things here so much.

If you have a negative image of your father, then it is not totally your father's fault. Just remember that he also was negatively influenced by your grandfather! A bad cycle repeats from generation to generation! Friend, perhaps you might ask me why you are in such a bad cycle which is neither your will nor your choice. A good question to ask indeed! To my knowledge, it is a consequence of humanity's sin so-called 'the Fall of man.' Please allow me to tell you what it is and how it happened.

***

The Bible describes that humanity was created in God's own image and designed to live a life of intimate fellowship with Him. God fashioned the first man, Adam from the earth something like this:

God formed Adam from the ground and breathed into his nostrils the breath of life, and he became a living creature. Then, He placed Adam in the Garden of Eden to till it and keep it and told him that he could eat from ANY tree in the garden except for one - the tree of the knowledge of good and evil at the centre of the garden. God also told him that the consequence for doing so would be to surely die. After the creation of Adam, God said that it was not good for *man* to be alone, so He created the first woman, Eve (Ḥawwāh in Hebrew, meaning 'living one') from Adam's rib. Friend, pay attention here! I didn't use the man but used the representative noun *man* which means all human beings. Someone jokingly said that men have one less rib bones than women's due to this surgery. Do you think so? Silly! People are born with 12 pairs of ribs, for a total of 24, no matter their sex. Actually, researchers reveal our ribs re-grow if damaged because the rib periosteum has a remarkable ability to regenerate bones. Anyway again it clearly shows that we are created for relationship! Otherwise why would He make Eve in the first place! After creating the man and the woman, God blessed them both and told them to be fruitful and multiply with dominion over the earth. They were perfect beings at that time.

Then (ta-da!) the serpent in the garden, which was described as craftier than any other beast of the garden, approached Eve. He tempted her saying that God was withholding from them by not letting them eat from the tree of the knowledge of good and evil. Friend, have you noticed that they had the ability to talk to animals here? Wow! When did humanity lose this ability? Please let me carry on and then you would know why we lost it. The serpent persuaded her that if they would eat the fruit from the tree that they would become like God. In case (if you don't know), Friend, I tell you the serpent was *Satan* in disguise. He had already been thrown down from God's place (Heaven) because of his rebellion towards God. Sadly, Eve ate the fruit from the tree and then gave the fruit to Adam and he ate it, too. At this moment, known as the fall of mankind, the original sin entered the world. With this reason humanity lost our supernatural ability (including talking to the animal) and became a slave of sin. Sigh!

***

Friend, it is a tragic incident in history just like 'no use crying over spilt milk!' No one on the earth could reverse it. Sounds like it, doesn't it? Hold on for a moment! Here is good news: it was not over yet! God had a plan for this hopelessly ruined humanity. He sent His most beloved and favourite one who could do His rescue plan for mankind. Can you guess who that person was? If you said, 'Jesus,' then you are correct. If you missed it, never mind.

Actually, his name is 'Yeshua' in Hebrew, meaning 'deliverer' or 'saviour.' Did you ask me why his name was changed into Jesus? Well, when Yeshua is first translated into Greek which the New Testament is derived from, it becomes Iēsous which in English spelling is Jesus. Friend, what do you feel if someone from a different culture calls you with a different name, claiming that your name is called in that way in his or her culture? For instance, you are 'John' but a German calls you 'Johannes.' Do you feel odd? Aha! With this reason I personally prefer Yeshua to Jesus if the person whom I talk to knows about it. By the way do you know that Yeshua is a pretty common name in Jewish society like 'John' or 'Rob' or 'Martin' here? If you wouldn't know the meaning of Yeshua, then you might wonder why he had such a common name rather than a royal name for a boy like Charles, William, George, Edward, Louis, Arthur, etc.. Do you know the meaning of your name? Naming a boy or a girl in certain culture is very important since it connotes a specific meaning related to his or her future destiny.

It is very true with the Jewish culture. Do you know a Jewish man called Abraham? He is known as the founding father of Judaism, Christianity and Islam. Originally, his name was Abram, meaning 'exalted father.' From the moment his name was changed into Abraham, meaning 'father of multitude,' he indeed became the father of many nations. Abraham's wife name was also changed from Sara (meaning my princess) to Sarah (meaning princess). She was no longer a possession but became Abraham's equal, i.e. being the princess of many nations. Also, the miracle baby of 100-year-old Abraham and 90-year-old Sarah was Isaac (meaning laughter). According to the biblical narrative, Abraham fell on his face and laughed when God imparted the news of their son's eventual birth since he well and truly passed human age to produce a baby and so did his wife Sarah. As his name means, Isaac indeed brought a joy to his family. This shows why naming a baby with a good meaning is so important. We unconsciously and continuously bless or curse him or her by calling someone with his or her name. Think about it: when people called Abraham, he kept hearing it and was reminded of 'who he was - the father of many nations.' Therefore, he became exactly *what he was called* continuously throughout his whole life until his death.

One of twelve apostles/disciples of Jesus was Matthew. He wrote the first book of the New Testament in the Bible. He used to be a tax-collector but became a follower of Jesus after encountering him. He was very rich but was hated by his own people because he worked for Herod Antipas, the tetrarch of Galilee who was the enemy of Jews around that time. He used to be called Levi (meaning *as taken up*) but became well known as Apostle Matthew (meaning *God's gift*) later on. His life was totally changed after he accepted Jesus' invitation to be his follower. Of course the price that he paid to follow him was all his wealth and the tax-collecting job which could guarantee a lifelong fortune. Truly he lived his life as God's gift for many just like the name of Matthew. I believe that by now you fully understand why naming someone with a good meaning is so important in this respect.

Let's go back to Yeshua. As his name implies, he came to the earth to do Father's rescue mission. Actually, his name was already given by angel Gabriel prior to his birth. He was born with that destiny indeed. Thankfully he completed his mission successfully and went back to where he came from. Friend, shall I remind you of my daydreaming that I came here to do His mission? Perhaps we can pause here for a moment and think about this seriously: why are you here on the earth?

***

It is not surprising to know that many people are struggling to connect with Father in Heaven because they don't have a good image of their earthly father here on the earth. I also had a father who had gone through tough times like a civil war and then poverty in his life time but achieved his wealth from scratch. How strong he was! Furthermore, he desired to have a son, but I was the number three among four girls in my family. Can you see what I am trying to say here? Frankly speaking, I also struggled to see Father in Heaven as a good one until I came to a point of knowing 'how good He is.' Of course, someone helped me see what a good father looks like. I do hope that it would help you as well.

A man called Abba had two sons, and his younger son asked him to give him his share of the wealth. Actually, it was very rude in their culture to request his inheritance before his father's death. Yet, Abba's younger son could not wait for his father's death and wanted it immediately. So, Abba agreed and divided his wealth between both sons.

Upon receiving his portion of the inheritance, the younger son travelled to a distant country and wasted all his money in extravagant living. Immediately thereafter, a famine did strike the land. He became desperately poor and was forced to take work as a swineherd. When he reached the point of envying the food of the pigs he was watching, he finally came to his senses. When he came to himself, he said to himself, 'How many hired servants of my father's have bread enough to eat. Yet, I perish with hunger

here! I will arise and go to my father, and will say to him: Father, I have sinned against Heaven, and before you, and am no more worthy to be called your son. Please make me as one of your hired servants.'
And then he arose, and was heading to his father's house. When he (younger son) was yet a great way off, Abba saw him, and had compassion, and ran, and fell on his neck, and kissed him. Abba even noticed him in the far distance because he was hopefully and eagerly watching for the son's return. Abba accepted him back wholeheartedly without hesitation before his son finished his rehearsed speech. On top of it, he called for his servants to dress his son in a fine robe, a ring, and sandals, and slaughter a fatted calf for a celebration in honour of his return, saying that 'My son was lost once but is found now. Rejoice with me!'

Is that not beautiful, Friend? This is the utterly most inspiring and heartfelt story I have ever heard of. Imagine that if you are a father to a son like Abba's younger one, what would be your response to him when he returns to you after he absolutely went broke? Have you had such a good father in your life? You did? Bless you! If you haven't had one, don't worry, Friend. Here is good news for you: let me introduce you to one like Abba. Father in Heaven is the one whom you are looking for. Run to Him, run into His arms and fall into grace, Friend. His mercy is calling out now. Don't refuse it. Don't hesitate. Just fall into His grace.

♥ Pause and Write Your Thoughts So Far

Two

You Name Must Be Holy

When was the last time you heard of swearwords or you swore at someone? Pardon me? Did you say that you did it today? Actually, I heard swearwords from someone on the street yesterday. Somehow (whether we hate it or not) we are bombarded by those words, aren't we?

Have you ever thought of 'why people swear'? Some say that they cannot stop it and even hard to talk to people without swearwords since they become so natural and are part of their speech just like 'old habits die hard.' Those words are used to vent (usually) bad emotion. If you think of them (not in detail), they include private parts, bodily functions, sex, anger, dishonesty, drunkenness, madness, disease, death, dangerous animals, fear, religion and so on and so forth. The swearwords, which are related to profanity, are called as curse (cuss) words, dirty words, foul words, bad words, and obscene words, etc.. The common denominator of them is *nothing good about it*. We'd better to raise our awareness and change our mindset if we are very accustomed to them. Actually, the Bible says about the power of the tongue: even death and life are in the power of the tongue although it is a small part of our body like a tiny spark which can set a great forest on fire. Powerful!

Look, having said that, some swearwords which include 'Jesus' and 'God.' They shouldn't be used in that way. Imagine that if your name could be used for the purpose of profanity, what do you feel? Then, why the names of God and Jesus are treated in that way? The greatest hater, *Satan* deceived people to use them for cursing and blaspheming the divinity in a distorted manner just like swearing which has a normal meaning of making a 'solemn promise' but becomes offensive.

***

Here I can tell you a real life changing story of a lady who is a single mum with a teenage boy. She dramatically became a believer of Jesus during her painful divorce process but could not stop swearing since she did it almost throughout her lifetime. Whenever she was angry at her son, she swore at him. One day she swore at her son as usual, and immediately she heard an inner voice, saying, 'Do you really want him to be like what you have just said?' She was struck and realised that she was cursing her son without thinking of it very much. Aha! It was part of her normal speech indeed! Certainly, it was her life changing moment. Immediately, she desperately cried, 'God, Help me! I pray.' She said that she didn't swear any longer when the supernatural power came upon her as she prayed.

Friend, now you realise how dangerous and powerful our tongue is. So stop using your tongue from evil and kill that old habit if you have! If you cannot help it, then why don't you ask God for a help? Please read the following prayer aloud from your heart as you really mean it. The supernatural power of God will definitely set you free from it if you simply believe it and trust Him.

Dear God,
I'm terribly sorry that I swore and
blasphemed you with my tongue.
Please forgive me and deliver me.
Destroy my old habit.
Cleanse my dirty mouth and
fill me with your Spirit and
set me free with Your power.
Thank you, God.
I pray this in Jesus' name.
Amen.

Not surprisingly, we don't hear the word 'holy' very much apart from an evil purpose of profanity like 'holy cow', 'holy molly', 'holy smoke' and so on and so forth, do we? Even then, do we really understand what holy means exactly? It's very abstract, isn't it? Let's get some help from a dictionary. It is defined as 'spiritually perfect or pure' according to *Collins English Dictionary*. Have you ever met a single person who is perfect or pure here on the earth? If you can find one, please let me know about it.

For some time, I had been intriguing and pondering about an interesting statement in the Bible: 'Be holy as I (God) am holy.' Let's think about this together for a moment. God certainly knows that we cannot be holy, yet commands us to be holy. Is he nasty to say that? Or is he cheeky to see that we cannot be holy utterly so he made us guilty about it? What do you think? I'm not God so I don't know what exactly His intention is but at least I can tell this to help your understanding. He wants us to be a *weak* but *clean* vessel so that His holiness can flow from us. Let me elaborate this a bit more.

First, let's focus on *weakness*. Imagine that you are a toddler who needs your parents' help most of your time. Your parents love you so much and want you to be proud of yourself. So they have decided to give you a job which you cannot do alone. Yet, you would think that you are doing well without realising that most of the job is unnoticeably done by them. Here is a key: your vulnerability requires your parents' help. Your parents are delighted to do so because they love you and want you to be proud of yourself by accomplishing the work together.

Now let's turn to *cleanness*. Imagine that you are a cook and have just finished cooking your gourmet food. And then you are looking for a plate. Do you think that you get a dirty plate for your food? Absolutely not! You definitely need a clean plate to display your food. Right! Now let's put these two concepts together: weakness and cleanness with which God can pour out His holiness on us. When we receive His holiness from above, then we can release it. I wonder whether it would help you understand better if I share this with you.

I love to go out almost every day if the weather permits here in the UK. One afternoon while walking on Welland river bank in Spalding, Lincolnshire, I saw a full circle rainbow. Indeed, it was interesting to see 'how it formed in a circle' as opposed to a half-full circle rainbow as usual. I have never seen a full circle rainbow before in my real life. Anyway the half of the rainbow above the river was the real one whereas the other half (lower part of the circle) was its reflection, yet it became a full circle rainbow together. Cool, isn't it? Supposedly we are a vessel to reflect God's holiness. The clearer we are, the more beautiful His holiness in us can be seen by others. The purer the river is, the more vivid the rainbow reflection is. So the purer our heart is, the clearer holiness can be reflected through us. I do hope that it makes sense to you. In brief, God wants all of us to live a pure and holy life to reflect a beauty in His holiness through us. Then how should we live? It is absolutely up to us!

♥ Pause and Write Your Thoughts So Far

Three

Your Kingdom Come

We are living in both the physical and the spiritual worlds. The former is visible whereas the latter is invisible but heavily influences the former. Even people who claim themselves as atheists say that they don't believe the spiritual world yet can experience some kind of spiritual things beyond human understanding and descriptions. Friend, the spiritual world is the reality whether you believe it or not. Just like the wind which you cannot see but acknowledge it when a tree is swayed by it. It is the same with the spiritual world: you cannot see spiritual forces with your physical eyes but acknowledge them because they greatly influence your physical world even if you deny them or are not aware of them.

"If you know the enemy and know yourself,
you need not fear the result of a hundred battles.
If you know yourself but not the enemy,
for every victory gained you will also suffer a defeat."

Sun Tzu, The Art of War

What Sun Tzu says here is very important in terms of 'warfare.' You may wonder why I am talking about it suddenly. Please allow me to tell you about it.

Warfare is real in the spiritual realm whether you are aware of it or not. All of us have experienced the spiritual forces in some degree, yet many of us ignore them due to a lack of knowledge. However, it is very real and undeniable with those who are seeking for the ultimate meaning of life which only can be found in the spirit world and also have experienced a kind of spiritual phenomena from it.

Indeed, there are two kingdoms in the spiritual realm: one is the kingdom of Darkness and the other is the kingdom of Light. The former is evil whereas the latter is good, yet both are influencing the physical world where we live in as mentioned earlier. Just as darkness and light are complete opposites, so are these two kingdoms. Do you remember what happened to the (physical) world when the original sin entered into it? All things became corrupt and ruined, hence even our minds and consciences became corrupted, too. What did the very first human beings, Adam and Eve do when the Sin conquered them? Well, they first tried to hide their shame by means of covering their private parts with leafy things and avoiding having their daily fellowship with God. Then, God asked Adam with a rhetorical question, 'Where are you?' What He tried to say to Adam here is that 'you know what you have done and hence you have hid yourself from Me.' God is still asking the same question to the human being (like you) who is lost and has not found the Way yet. 'Where are you?'

***

Do you know why people deny God's existence? I can tell you the reason: we have an issue related to the Sin. Perhaps you may argue with me saying that you have never been in jail with crimes. Hold on! What I'm saying here is the original sin and our sinful nature. Again you might say that you didn't commit the original sin. It is their fault. Correct! Unfortunately, this sin has been inherited like DNA from one generation to the next generation. So none of us are exceptional! Is that unfair? That's the consequence of the Sin which we are bearing or suffering from. Also, that is why the darkness can so powerfully influence us. They have legally gotten leeway to attack us violently. I can tell you more about this from my experience.

***

I met a lady called Dinah (name changed) who knew Jesus and also was involved in the New Age occult practices such as tarot card reading, astrology, yoga, meditation techniques, and mediumship, etc.. According to the New Age practitioners, these practices are integrated into the new age movement as tools to assist personal transformation. A form of their spirit mediumship is called 'channelling' which is a hyper-individualised religiosity. In general, New Agers claim that an individual can create his or her own reality through it.

Actually, a friend of my husband and me who knew Dinah first introduced her to us and asked us whether we could help her. At that time she was suffering from the dark forces after she was involved in such occult practices. Dinah told us that she actually talked to her dead husband, and even her husband soothed her while channelling. While we were talking to her about the kingdom of Light (God's goodness) and its virtue (i.e. peace and joy in the Spirit of God), the dark forces began to manifest by means of changing her voice (sounds very likely a masculine voice). We knew that we have the authority over the dark forces, so we commanded the dark spirit to leave from her. We clearly noticed that the two kingdoms were fighting in her at the moment. Immediately, in the spiritual world I was able to see a little girl Dinah and Jesus who was in front of her with his open arms in a room. I asked her, 'Dinah, can you see the light in front of you now?' 'Yes,' she said. 'It's Jesus. He is calling you out from the darkness. Come to him,' I said. There was a resistance from her for a moment. Yet, when the light (Jesus) became stronger and stronger, she couldn't resist it anymore. She (figuratively) grabbed Jesus' hands and then the peace came upon her from above. At last, the kingdom of Light won!

Friend, this is a tug of war battle between the two kingdoms which I talked about earlier. When the kingdom of Light is predominant, the kingdom of Darkness had to go. It's just like this: what would happen when you go into a dark room and then turn on a light? Immediately the room becomes full with the light and no darkness remains. That's the power of light!

***

From time to time I teamed up with a non-profit charity called, *Journey Into Wholeness* (JIW)[1]. JIW periodically do their (rescue) mission in *Spirit, Mind, Body Fair* throughout the year around Essex County. They hold a Christian stall there to reach out to spiritual seekers whenever the Fair is on. I do remember an interesting occurrence. While other team members were setting up, displaying and preparing the JIW stall, I was looking around the exhibition hall and noticed several spirit stalls and psychic mediums which were also ready for their clients. I heavily sensed the dark forces in the air as the sounds of a huge Buddhist's gong permeated the atmosphere at the hall. While I was standing in front of the JIW stall in order to make appointments for the clients, a lady in a diagonally opposite psychic stall stared at me although I

---

[1] JIW website: https://journeyintowholeness.co.uk

didn't pay attention to her very much. Later on I was told that the psychic couldn't read the mind of her clients on that day. It is obviously warfare between the two kingdoms. Friend, when the kingdom of Light prevails, the kingdom of Darkness cannot stand and must be defeated. You'd better choose which kingdom you should belong to.

***

My family had a wonderful opportunity to go to Mozambique, Africa. There is an orphanage and a school run by a missionary organisation called, *Iris Global*[2] in Pemba, the northern part of Mozambique. We were staying there for some months, and many remarkable things happened in the meantime. (If you are curious about other stories of my family, you can read my book, *Shofar-blowing: Sounds From Heaven To Earth* which is available to purchase in the forms of paperback and e-book on Amazon platform.) There were many people from different nations to do good works and help the community around the area. On weekends some of us as a team went to remote areas from the Iris Centre, camping in 'Bush-bush' (staying in an environment with no tap water and no electricity for the weekends) and blessing the people group (mainly the Makua tribe) around them. When you go to such a place as a stranger, somehow it is unavoidable to encounter either strange things or dangerous creatures or creepy people. Actually it happened to one of the teams. A shaman (witch doctor) came to their camping area with his magical pets, *adders* in order to threaten them, yet he had a powerful encounter of Jesus instead. He was delivered from the dark forces and was totally healed and even married afterwards. (Watch the remarkable story on YouTube titled *Former witch doctor shares testimony.*[3]) Of course, the adders were burnt in

---

[2] https://www.irisglobal.org/
[3] https://www.youtube.com/watch?v=SyIWjIIfzCA

the fire with his consent. Again, this is warfare between the two kingdoms, and you can see the power of the kingdom of Light defeats the kingdom of Darkness!

Now you understand the importance of knowing who your enemy is and where you are now. Perhaps it is time for you to decide which kingdom you should belong to. If you have been suffering from the dark forces not only mentally but also physically, why don't you ask God to set you free from that affliction? I am happy to help you out. Please pray aloud if possible from your heart (when you yourself can hear it, the enemy can hear it, too) and believe what you have prayed and wait until the Spirit of God (Holy Spirit) will come upon you with peace.

Father in heaven,
I'm terribly sorry that I didn't know You and Your kingdom
I've been in the darkness for a long time.
Please forgive me.
Set me free from the dark forces by Your Spirit right now.
I sincerely pray that Your kingdom come
in my body, soul, mind and spirit
in Jesus' name.
Amen.

♥ Pause and Write Your Thoughts So Far

Four

Your Will Be Done Here As It Is In Heaven

What is your understanding of 'will'? It is generally understood that if we have free will, then we are allowed to choose what we want. In practice, if we could legally make a will, we would write down what we want to have happened to our money and our stuff after death. It is very much related to 'want' and 'choice.' In this sense, please bear with me by asking, 'Will you be surprised to know that God also has a will (i.e. particular desire) for you?' What if His will is different from 'what you are now' or 'what you are thinking of yourself now' or 'what you do now'? It is a pretty serious question, isn't it? Please think about it seriously for a moment.

In the Bible, there is a scroll (or a book as a modern term) in Heaven written by (or for) your life. I'm not sure whether it is blank so that it will be written by what you are doing here on the earth or it was already written but erased and then replaced by what you have done. Anyway, 'what has been and will be recorded in it' is important, isn't it? Also, it is obvious that it is totally your choice! Imagine what if it was already written but erased and replaced by your selfish and ambitious will on the earth. Many people whom I know are continuously seeking God's will rather than their own will. I often hear from them asking, 'How do I know whether it is God's will if I would choose this or that?' It is undeniable that we have to constantly make choices throughout our life journey. As a matter of fact, we make choices with our own risk of failures after all, don't we? What do you do in the case of an 'either-or' decision (especially one is against the other)? Perhaps those who are seeking God's will in their choices (even if their choices look unfavourable from a human viewpoint) are smarter than those who simply do it according to their own will. Do you agree? If not, hold that thought for a moment.

***

Some years ago I met a young mum with a toddler at *Spirit, Mind, Body Fair* in Essex. Some of my likeminded friends prayed for me prior to the day as I was scheduled to keep the JIW stall for two hours. I would like to remind you again that it is warfare between the two kingdoms. I was preparing myself for the Fair and praying for people who would come on the following day. In the midst of the preparation I strangely heard a voice, 'Three fifteen.' I wondered what it meant although I could think of so many possible things related to that number.

It was a Saturday afternoon when I was supposed to do my job at the JIW stall. There was a hustle and bustle going on at the exhibition hall after lunch. Many were visiting and walking around the different stalls. I was quite busy to meet several clients at the stall. In the meantime I noticed the mum and her push chair next to my table inside the stall. So I politely told her, 'I nearly finished with this man so I can get you soon.' She said, 'No problem at all. I can wait here.' After I had done with the man, I asked her to come to the table where I was sitting. While she was taking a seat, I looked up at the big clock on the wall of the hall. To my surprise, it was exactly 3:15! I hold my breath for a second. I immediately recalled the number I heard the day before. 'Okay, God. Now I know what the number means. What do I have to say to this lady then?' I calmly opened up our conversation with general questions like whether it was her first visit to the Fair, and where she came from, and what brought her here, and so on. While conversing with her, I clearly understood why God had caught my attention by saying 'Three fifteen.' Indeed, she was brought up in a church community so she knew and witnessed the supernatural power like healing and miracles from her young age. Nevertheless, she drifted away from God as she had grown up. The reason that she came to the Fair was for her spiritual need. I told her about 'what she was really looking for and how to get it.' Also, I mentioned to her about 'her book' in Heaven and the number 'Three fifteen' which I mysteriously heard the day before. She was so touched and realised that the loving Father in Heaven still loved her and was waiting for her return. At the end of our lengthy conversation, she willingly gave up her will for God's will. I noticed that she had peace as she resumed her route by God's GPS (Global Positioning System). Bless her!

Here are our fundamental questions to ask: what and how do we know about our heavenly Father's will for us? If it might differ from our will, what should we do? Then, do we willingly give up ours for His? Well, it won't be easy, will it? Thus, would you say that He looks terrible to us? Our response totally depends on our trust in Him. You know someone very well in depth and then you decide whether you can trust or distrust him or her. Am I right? Friend, if you don't have a relationship with God, then you cannot trust Him and won't give up yours for His will. Do you think that He is so terrible and wants you to have a miserable life here? If you allow me, then I can tell you about a person who gave up everything for His will, yet he regained all later on.

From the very beginning this man was very rich and owned everything. He had an intimate relationship with his father. He was so dear to his father, so was his father dear to him. One thing bothered his father so much was: he had a great compassion on people whom he invested with all he had. Nevertheless, they were terrible to his father and even thoroughly evil by mocking and killing his father's messengers who continuously delivered his kind messages to them. One day his father asked his son whether he willingly would go to the place where the terrible people were with a risk of danger by delivering his message. His son loved his father so much and agreed to do so. He went to the place where the horrible people lived. He arrived there in disguise so only a few of them noticed that he was their master's son whereas the majority of them hardly knew who he was. The man tried to deliver his father's message as much as he could, yet they were so evil and rejected his message and even hated him. The worst thing was that the evil ones discussed with each other and decided to kill him for their own benefits. Their wicked plot was unfolded, and the man knew that he was about to die by the evil hands. He was in a dilemma, whether he would escape and save his life or complete his errand given by his beloved father with the cost of his death. He thought and thought again and finally made his decision in prayer: 'Father, not my will, but yours be done.' He laid down his life to complete his mission given by his father.

Wait! It is not the end of his story. He came to life after three days when the power of life raised him from death. He once gave up everything and even his life, but he regained all humanity with the price of his death - that was the price which the enemy asked for! He gave up his will for his father's will so that all humanity can be saved from the enemy's hand. He is an outstanding example to show *why it is so significant to give up our will for our Father's will*. When we give up ours,

Father God can do what He wants to do through us. Friend, why don't you say this with me:

Father in Heaven,
not my will, but yours be done
as you planned.
I ask this in Jesus' name.
Amen.

♥ Pause and Write Your Thoughts So Far

Five

Give Us Today Our Daily Needs

Nowadays we often hear that we are living in an unprecedented time after the COVID-19 pandemic broke out as its name says it happened globally in 2019 and lasted for some time. The pandemic has impacted all aspects of society: schools closed across the world, businesses closed which caused many people to lose their jobs, social distancing and the national lockdowns worldwide. Consequently, not only a health crisis but also an economic crisis arose seriously. Sadly, domestic abuse and family violence increased around the world during lockdowns. Divorce rates and the percentage of suicide deaths escalated, too. What a remarkable time we live in! There is no doubt that those who had gone through difficult times in their life time like the world wars and foreign invasions would adopt their war strides once again. Even it became worse for those who have suffered from hunger as they were facing double crises. One thing for sure is that most of us felt insecure as we faced an uncertain future like this. When it comes to the matter of our essential needs especially our daily meals, it becomes a big issue because it is much related to our survival.

I do remember that my parents had gone through such tough times and told me how hungry they were when they were young. Their only wish they had at the time was 'if we could eat our food without worries.' Although they told me and my siblings about their tough life in the past from time to time, we were not in tune with them so much and haven't had such experience, either. Nevertheless, the majority of my parents' generation were the victim of both the war and the foreign invasions. Hence, they even lost their opportunity of education so they only could afford to get low paying jobs consequently. I do remember a few of my classmates came to school without their packed lunch and filled their empty stomach with water during the lunchtime. My schoolmate Sunny who was the eldest of many children in her poor family became a nanny for a teacher's baby. The teacher knew about her situation and willingly took her home as a nanny so that she could live at least without worrying about food, clothing and housing.

I also remember an old lady Momo and her grandson of a poor family. I don't know whether other family members were with her at that time. Anyway my mother is a very generous, charitable and godly woman. One day she asked me whether I could visit Momo with her to deliver a sack of rice (about 9-10 kg). I had never met her before but agreed to go since the sack of rice was quite heavy to carry alone so I could give her a hand if needed. Actually, Momo lived in a shabby house standing on a hilly side of the barren and stony field. I knew why my mother asked me to accompany her while we were walking a long distance with the sack of rice. My mother knocked on the door which was almost falling apart. A little old lady Momo came out to welcome us. Literally, she was very small and skinny and had a deeply tanned skin due to the strong sunshine while working at her vegetable field where she grew some vegetables to sell on an open-market. When my mother told her that we came to give away the sack of rice, she was so thrilled and thankful saying, 'We ate up the flour yesterday and have nothing to eat today.' She was really touched and repeatedly thanked us. I don't know whether she prayed for her daily provision for tomorrow the day before, but we were there to meet her desperate need for the next day onwards. Amazing!

On the way back home, I asked my mother how she knew that Momo needed daily food. She told me that while she was thinking of Momo, she had a strong impression that she was in desperate need of food. My mother often experienced such feelings (very unusual but strong feelings), then she acknowledged that it was from God for someone who was in need. Of course, she didn't ignore that feeling and exactly did what she felt. I believe that God used her to meet Momo's need because He knew that my mother would do whatever He would ask her to help others with her generosity. She was a channel of blessing to Momo indeed. Is that not cool? God hears and sees someone's needs and uses others to meet their necessity.

***

Now I love to share my own experience with you. It certainly tells you about how God exactly hears and sees someone's needs and uses others to meet their needs. As mentioned earlier, my family went to Mozambique and stayed there for some time. After we came back home, we didn't have regular income and almost used up our savings for that trip. Nevertheless, I don't deny that it was our family adventure. We experienced many exciting things while we were there. You can also find amazing stories in my book, *Shofar-Blowing: Sounds From Heaven To Earth.*

This is a story after that trip. It was a difficult time we had to go through until my husband Peter would get a full time job again. In the meantime, we had to live with what was available on a daily basis. Occasionally we had to live with only a loaf of bread (a reduced priced loaf from a supermarket if we were fortunate!) One late Saturday afternoon, Peter suggested to me whether I could accompany him to fix an old gentleman's TV with a cable. I don't usually go with him for such an occasion but strangely thought that I could accompany him at that time. After he got the TV cable, we drove to this gentleman's house where the rich people lived around that area. When we got there, he and his wife just finished unloading the items from their grocery shopping bags and boxes. They said that they had bought so many vegetables from the reduced shelves which they may not finish them all in time. So they asked us whether we would like to have some of them. We thanked them for their kindness. When we were about to leave their place after Peter fixed his TV, we saw a bagful of vegetables in a grocery bag - it was a sufficient amount for a week! I have something to tell you, Friend. On that day (Yes, I never forget that day. It was the day that I went to a supermarket with a pound coin and came out with the loaf of bread from the reduced self.) I looked up to Heaven and said, 'Don't make my life miserable again!' Yes, He heard it and surprised me with the bagful of vegetables - I didn't even ask for!

***

This is a real story which had happened in the Middle East a long time ago. A boy and his mother were kicked out from his father's house. She was an Egyptian maidservant and a surrogate mother in his father's household. When his half brother was born from his father's wife (step mother to him), they had to leave the house due to the conflict between his half brother and him. On the day of their leaving, his father prepared some food and a skin of water for them and then sent them off. They wandered in the desert for some time. When the water in the skin was gone, his mother put him under one of the bushes, and then she went off and sat down about a bowshot away and thought, 'I cannot watch my boy die.' And she began to sob as she sat there. At that moment, God heard the boy crying and sent his angel to them. The angel of God said to her, 'Don't be afraid. God has heard the boy crying as he lies there. So lift the boy up and take him by the hand for I will make him into a great nation.' And then she saw a well of water nearby. She ran to the well and filled the skin with water and gave the boy a drink. In their desperate need, God heard their cry and met their need. Indeed, I heard many stories like this - *how God miraculously provided.*

Friend, I don't know what you are struggling with at the moment, yet I truly encourage you to pause here for a moment and pray as below. Trust Him and believe that it will be done to you as you pray. Who knows it will be your wonderful story to tell others later on?

Father in Heaven,
I have just read such wonderful stories.
Please do the same miracle in my life.
Hear my cry.
Give me _____ (say what you need).
Thank you.
I ask this in Jesus' name.
Amen.

Friend, do you know that a charitable heart always touches God's heart? Please allow me to tell you a story which would help you understand it better. Did you say, 'A story again!'? I love telling stories because they inspire me so much.

Cornelius was a centurion whose position was in the Roman army during classical antiquity, nominally the commander of 100 soldiers. He and all his family were devout and God-fearing. He gave generously to those in need and prayed to God regularly. One afternoon during his prayer time as usual, an angel visited him in his vision (i.e. religious ecstasy) and instructed him to invite a Jewish church leader called Simon Peter home for a house gathering. The angel also told him where he could find Simon Peter. Around that era, the Jews were culturally not associated with the Romans because they regarded them as their enemy who invaded and conquered them. It was against the Jewish law, too. Actually, Cornelius was a highly respected commander by both the Jews and the Romans. According to the Angel's instruction, he sent off his two servants along with a soldier to get Simon Peter.

In the meantime, Simon Peter also saw all manner of beasts and fowls being lowered from Heaven in a sheet in his vision. A voice commanded him to eat, but he objected to eating those animals which were unclean according to the Jewish law. The voice told him not to call unclean that which God has cleansed. When Cornelius' men arrived, Simon Peter clearly understood that through this vision God wanted him to tell 'the word of God' to the non-Jewish people. Otherwise, he definitely wouldn't go to Cornelius' house because it was against the Jewish law.

While Cornelius was waiting, he had called his kinsmen and near friends to come for the house gathering. When Simon Peter arrived at Cornelius' house, they were ready to hear the word of God. As he spoke to them about Jesus' work and his resurrected life after death, the Spirit of God (Holy Spirit) descended on everyone at the place. Hence, all of them were baptized. [Baptism is a religious rite by means of submerging in water and coming up out of it for purification in Spirit.] This event became well-known as the first non-Jewish believers of Jesus in history.

It is fascinating to see how God works with people to meet other's needs and rewards those who show their generosity and kindness to others. Actually, the English word, *company* means the condition of being with others. It is originally from Latin: 'com-' meaning 'with together', and '-panis' means 'bread.' It implies that in order to keep our good relationship with others, something we can share with them is basically 'breads.' In other words, the best way to show our genuine concern to others is to meet their desperate need like 'breads.' Fascinating!

Friend, are you worrying about your daily necessity now? Here is good news for you. The Bible says that we do not worry about our life, what we will eat or drink; or about our body, what we will wear. As I see birds in my garden and in the air, they don't seem to worry about their food even they do not sow or reap or store away in barns because there are many berries on trees and grains on the fields around here. Also, I see how flowers of the garden and the field grow. They are here today but will be gone tomorrow. Even they do not labour or spin to clothe themselves. Yet, they are beautiful because Father in Heaven clothes them.

Have you seen a 'Rafflesia arnoldii' which holds the record of the world's largest bloom of the flower? This rare flower is found in the rainforests of Indonesia. It can grow to be 3 feet across and weigh up to 15 pounds! Or have you seen a 'Titan arum' which is also known as the 'corpse flower' for its odour regardless of its vivid purple colour. The Titan arum is not a single flower but a cluster of many tiny flowers although it looks like a single giant flower. It can reach heights of 7 to 12 feet and weigh as much as 170 pounds!

I am always fascinated by the vivid and colourful feathers of birds. For example, look at the feathers of macaws. They are considered as the largest species of very colourful parrots in the world. How about the national bird of India, the 'Indian Peacock' which astonishes people for ages with their beauty? Their tail feathers making up about 60% of bird's length are incredibly gorgeous. No wonder why Jesus said that even Solomon with his riches was not dressed as beautifully as flowers (and even birds).

Again the Bible also says that we don't need to worry about 'what shall we eat?' or 'what shall we drink?' or 'what shall we wear?' because Father in Heaven knows that we need them. Surely He gives us what we need if we would ask because He is a good Father.

♥ **Pause and Write Your Thoughts So Far**

Six

Forgive Our Sins As We Forgive Those Who Sin Against Us

'A person who is forgiven little shows only little love whereas those with many sins have been forgiven are able to love God more.'

Yeshua the Nazarene

'Forgiveness is the fragrance that the violet sheds on the heel that has crushed it.'

Mark Twain

I have paraphrased a profound statement of Yeshua (Jesus) here. What do you think about that? Before telling me your thought, please let me ask you this question: why would or should we forgive someone who has wronged us in the past?

Forgiveness is psychologically defined as a *conscious, deliberate decision* to release the feelings of resentment or vengeance towards a person or a group who has emotionally (and physically) harmed us. Is there a reward for 'letting go of a painful past'? According to *the Art of Forgiveness* by Lewis B. Smedes (1996), to forgive means releasing ourselves from past incidents and the people who have hurt us, indicating that we are ready to move on and embrace the present moment.

Many psychologists claim that in the physical domain forgiveness is associated with lower heart rate and blood pressure, and reducing fatigue, and increasing sleep quality. In the psychological domain, it diminishes the experience of stress and inner conflict by simultaneously restoring positive thoughts, feelings, and behaviours. Actually, people with mental illnesses can experience a range of physical symptoms such as muscle tension, pain, headaches, insomnia, and feelings of restlessness from the perspective of clinical psychologists. It has been known as *psychosomatic disorders* (i.e. emotional stress manifests in the body as physical pain and other symptoms) which mainly result from stress. I personally saw it with my own eyes.

***

A mid-aged lady who is a talented musician and especially very good at African drumming asked my husband and me for healing prayer. We had known her for some years. She often ran drum workshops for folks who were curious and interested in learning drumming. One day I asked her how her workshop went. Then she said to me that she couldn't do it due to the severe pain on her chest so her colleague took it over instead. What a pity! With that news we scheduled to meet up with her. She told us how the pain began. From our experiences, one thing for sure is that it is very important to know someone's life story and background in relation to healing process. While listening to her, we understood an issue of a broken relationship between her and her brother for years. She was wounded by him and hadn't talked to him for a long time. We told her about the power of forgiving and then encouraged her to forgive her brother first prior to our healing prayer for her. She paused in silence for a while. (Friend, to forgive is a conscious, deliberate decision as mentioned earlier!) And then she consented to that saying aloud, 'I forgive Frank (name changed).' After she finished saying this, we prayed for healing. She burst into tears and cried, 'The pain had gone!' This is the lady of the husband who once suffered from DDD (Degenerative disk disease; When normal changes that take place in the disks of the spine, it causes pain) but was miraculously healed by God. You can also read her husband's amazing occurrence in my book, *Shofar-blowing: Sounds From Heaven To Earth*. Indeed, after she first experienced her healing, she requested us to help her husband as well.

The power of forgiveness! Jesus knew this and taught his followers: *forgive our sins as we forgive those who sin against us*. Here it implies that someone has hurt us first. That's right. He said 'as we forgive...' It is a *preceding action* prior to either our sins are forgiven or our healing happens. We saw many were healed after they forgave someone who had hurt them before. If you are physically (and emotionally) suffering now, please pause here and pray aloud as below:

Father in Heaven,
Please help me remember anyone
whom I need to forgive.

(Wait quietly and patiently until He reminds you of that person. Now continue to pray as below.)

I forgive _____ (someone's name).

(You can wait here if needed.
When you are ready, you continue to pray as below.)

Forgive all my sins and heal me
as I forgave _____ (someone's name).
Thank you.
I pray this in Jesus' name.
Amen.

Indeed, I have encountered so many people who were hurt by their family members and close friends. The majority of the wounded think that they would never forgive the people who hurt them - even think that they don't deserve forgiveness! It is quite challenging to forgive the person who has offended you and even move away from your role as victim by releasing the control and power of the offending person and situation have had in your life. I don't deny it, either. Interestingly, many writers talk about something like '7 steps to forgiveness', '15 steps to forgiveness' and '30 steps to forgiveness', etc.. If you have done it according to their advices and it worked with you, then it is absolutely fabulous. If you have done it but didn't work with you, then here is good news: to forgive our offender(s) totally depends on our mindset. Also, the Spirit of God (Holy Spirit) willingly enables us to do so if you would ask him for a help.

The prevalent obstacles to forgiveness are mainly 'I feel unready to forgive' and 'I shield myself from further harm.' We also resist forgiving because we don't want to feel our pain again because forgiveness requires that we get present to our suffering. There is an ongoing suffering for both parties when the issue of forgiveness is not resolved between them. What a pity!

Let us think about it the other way around for a moment. Imagine that you are the one who hurt someone but are forgiven by him or her (even you don't deserve forgiveness!). It is a different story now, isn't it? It might make you miserable if you were not forgiven and live the rest of your life with the guilty consciousness.

Jesus talks about an important point from a different perspective. If we forgive other people when they sin against us, Father in Heaven will also forgive us. This means that if we don't, Father in Heaven won't. Why did he say that? Let us hear his explanation from his parable (paraphrased as below):

> *A king wanted to settle accounts with his servants. As he began the settlement, a man called Aaric who owed him £40,000 was brought to him. Since he was not able to pay back, the king ordered that he and his wife and his children and all that he had be sold to repay the debt. At this Aaric fell on his knees before him and begged, 'Please be patient with me. I will pay back everything.' The king took pity on him, cancelled the debt and then let him go. While he was on his way, Aaric found one of his fellow workers who owed him £4,000. Aaric grabbed him and began to choke him. 'Pay back what you owe me!' he demanded. His fellow worker fell to his knees and begged him, 'Be patient with me, and I will pay it back.' But Aaric refused. Instead, he went off and had the man thrown into jail until he could pay the debt. When the other workers saw what had happened, they were outraged and went and told the king everything that had happened. Then the king called Aaric in. 'You wicked*

one,' he said, 'I cancelled all that debt of yours because you begged me to. Shouldn't you have had mercy on your fellow worker just as I had on you?' In anger the king handed him over to the jailer to be tortured, until he should pay back all he owed. Then Jesus concluded his parable by saying, 'This is how Father in Heaven will treat each of us unless we forgive our brother or sister from our heart.'

We need to pay attention to what Jesus said here. We should forgive others first so that we can be forgiven. The Bible also clearly says about it.

"

**If you forgive those who sin against you,
your heavenly Father will forgive you.
But if you refuse to forgive others,
your Father will not forgive your sins.**

"

I learned this from my own experiences when I prayed for others' healing. I love to hear their stories when I was asked for healing prayer. While listening, I could understand the root of the physical condition/sickness. I have found that the bottom line of their sickness mainly resulted from their unforgiveness underneath. When they forgave their offender, the healing always happened after prayer. That is the power of forgiving! Also, the Bible clearly says, 'Bear with each other and forgive one another if any of you has a grievance against someone.'

I love the following story so much because his life was so colourful and showed us what true meaning of forgiveness against envy, betrayal, fear, temptation, rejection and accusation. Through the tough life training, he eventually learned the beauty of forgiveness.

He was one of his father's 12 sons -number 11. All of his older brothers were half-brothers from different mothers except his younger brother. You can picture what family he was born into. His father loved him more than any of the others and even gave him a special coat. Being given a special coat would have only fuelled the brothers' jealousy.

The choice of colours in the coat held great prestige in the ancient world around his time. The vivid colours like red and purple were held in high esteem because it was very costly to create the dyes. Thus, his red and purple coat reinforced the message to his brothers that he was his father's favourite. On top of this, he was a big dreamer and bragged about it. Due to his father's favouritism and his attitude towards his brothers, his brothers were jealous of him and eventually sold him into slavery. When he was 17 years old, he was taken to Egypt from his homeland and became a slave to Potiphar (the captain of the ancient Egyptian ruler, Pharaoh's guard). Potiphar's wife tried unsuccessfully to seduce him because he was a smart and good-looking man. Yet, he refused her tempt and ended up with imprisonment after her false accusation. Due to his ability to interpret Pharaoh's dream, he became the second-in-command in Egypt later on. He wisely managed the country's produce in preparation for a time of famine not only in Egypt but also the neighbouring countries.

During the famine, his brothers came to Egypt to plead with him for food supplies. Time passed so his brothers did not recognise him at all in the first place. He tested out whether they were changed or still the same as before. He identified himself as their younger brother with great joy after he was satisfied with the fact that his brothers were not the same as before. He invited his father and brothers to come and settle in Egypt where he took care of them.

When his father passed away, his brothers worried that his younger brother might hold a grudge against them so he would pay them back for all the wrongs they did to him. Here he treated his brothers nicely and spoke kindly, 'You intended to harm me, but God intended it for good to accomplish what is now being done, the saving of many lives. So don't be afraid. I will provide for you and your children.'

He was betrayed and sold, falsely accused and forgotten which were his setbacks to deal with in his lifetime. Nevertheless, he did not become embittered but overcame. In the process of these experiences he learned and helped people including his brothers who treated him badly before. He truly forgave his brothers. This is the beauty of forgiveness!

Indeed, he was the well-known and second-in command in Egypt, Joseph. He was a real person in both Israeli and Egyptian histories. Actually his story is well-known from the Bible. The events of his life are also found in the Torah (the first part of the Jewish Bible) and the Qur'an (the sacred text of Islam). From the history record, we can understand that his story begins in Canaan (modern day Palestine, Syria and Israel) around 1600 to 1700 BC. I personally believe that he became well-known throughout history because he first learned to forgive so that he could save his people from the famine.

Jesus himself learned to forgive others, too. When the Roman soldiers crucified him (an ancient punishment; Putting someone to death by nailing or binding them to a cross) at the place called the Skull (skull-shaped hill in ancient Jerusalem) and gambled for his clothes by throwing dice, he said, 'Forgive them, Father because they don't know what they are doing.'

It sounds like that all of us must learn to forgive during our lifetime, doesn't it? Well, I guess that if we have learned to forgive, then that could be the greatest gift we can get here on the earth. If you disagree, then I will leave that to you.

♥ **Pause and Write Your Thoughts So Far**

Seven

Do Not Let Us Yield To Temptation

A boy was asked to house-sit as the owner of the house was away for a while. He was told that he could touch anything in the house. However, one thing he was not allowed to touch was the bird cage at the particular area. Yes, the bird cage! He was not told the reason although the house owner sternly and repeatedly told him not to touch it. A day passed. Two days passed... And as time went, the boy became gradually curious about what bird was inside the cage and rationally thought that perhaps the bird might need food and water. As soon as he opened the door of the cage, the bird HOPE was banished in the blink of eye.

This is an allegory that I heard of a long time ago. I think that it exactly shows what our nature would be when a temptation comes to us and no one is around us. Let's think about what temptations that we hardly resist, and then why we cannot resist them.

Do you remember how the original sin entered into humanity? When the serpent tempted the first female human Eve in the Garden of Eden, (to her) the fruit of the tree was *good for food* (i.e. the lust of the flesh in other words) and *pleasing to the eye* (i.e. the lust of the eyes), and also *desirable for gaining wisdom* (i.e. pride of life). This exactly presents three main areas that we love in the world and hardly resist them when we were offered to have them. The serpent knows the weakness of humanity which can be easily attacked and destroyed. So he constantly does this to everyone throughout the human history. I said, 'Everyone.' Certainly, no one is exempted from temptations! What makes us different is whether we can resist them or give in to them. It is simple but very challenging!

Psychologists say that three areas in our life which we are longing for all the time are: *hedonism, egoism* and *materialism*. They are fancy names, aren't they? Let us look at each of them briefly.

The word 'Hedonism' comes from the ancient Greek for 'pleasure.' So it is defined as pursuit of pleasure, especially to the pleasures of the senses. Sense pleasure is basically any pleasing that comes from one of the five senses (sight, hearing, touch, smell, and taste) - for examples, watching a film, listening to music, reading books, eating desserts, etc..

In psychoanalytic theory, the word 'Ego' is a portion of the human personality addressed as the 'self.' 'Egoism' means that individual self-interest which is the actual motive of all conscious action.

'Materialism' is the constant concern over material possessions and wealth. Thus, worldly concerns (goods and

51

wealth) are the most important things over spiritual or intellectual values. Valuing a new car over friendships is an example of materialism. Some researchers say that materialism reflects a value system that is preoccupied with *possessions* and the *social image* which the individual projects.

Are they all bad or good? You might be right if you would say that it depends on 'to some degree.' Then, can you tell me 'what degree' is bad or good? We do have desire for pleasure, self-image and needs for possessions, don't we? The point is that it becomes bad when they excessively occupy us. Do you agree?

Let us take examples each. It is alright to have a desire of pleasure but is bad to pursuit for the lust (strong desire) of the flesh. There is nothing wrong with having an ego, that is, there is nothing wrong with feeling important. However, the problems arise when the ego affects our decision making, our mood, or it turns us into a victim, an underdog, or it makes us feel superior to others in order to justify our behaviour. The major pitfall of materialism is that we define our value in terms of the objects we own and even judge others based on their earnings and financial status. Now you might ask me a question, 'Is it possible not to fall into a temptation?' Holding answering to your question, will it surprise you if I would say that Jesus was tempted three times in these three areas? Let me remind you that the first human beings failed. Right? And then did Jesus fail as well? Let us see what happened to him.

The Spirit of God (Holy Spirit) led Jesus into the desert to be tempted by the devil. Please don't ask me why the Spirit of God did it. After forty days and nights without food, Jesus was very hungry. I guess he could eat a horse by then. The devil came to him and tempted him to turn stones into breads. It is the temptation for the pleasure of food. To this temptation, Jesus responded to him that humanity needs higher value than the food. 'Man cannot live on bread alone, but needs every word God speaks.'

The second temptation was for Jesus to throw himself from the highest point of the temple and order angels to catch him with their hands. This is the temptation for the egoism. Jesus responded to him that God should be the first rather than himself. 'Do not put your God to the test.'

The final temptation was that the devil offered Jesus all the kingdoms of the world in return for worshipping him. This is the temptation for materialism. If he would worship him (the devil), then he could possess all that the world could offer. Nevertheless, the response of Jesus was so solid and clear because he knew that the only one to worship must be the God almighty. 'Worship your God and serve only him!'

Have you noticed how Jesus won the battle of temptation above? If you did, then I can cheer you up, 'Bravo!' If you didn't, never mind. I tell you his secret weapons that knocked out the enemy.

If you look at the last sentence of each paragraph again, it ends with a citation in quotation marks. It implies that Jesus responded to each temptation with the word from the Torah (the first part of the Jewish Bible), especially the book of Deuteronomy in the Old Testament. This clearly shows that when he was tempted and fell in a difficult situation, he followed God's word for guidance. What amazes me most is that he cited all those words from his memory. I reckon that he read the Torah many times or had a very good memory to remember God's word that he read. Anyway he used one of the secret weapons very well and eventually won the battle.

The other secret weapon was his powerful prayer! Let me remind you that Jesus was in the desert without food for forty days and nights. Indeed, he was in fasting (a religious observance, abstaining from all or some kinds of food or drink) and praying during the time. How he did it? Well, it is hard for a human being without the help of the Spirit of God. He was prayerful prior to the temptation. This is the power of prayer which helps us to resist the temptation.

One of Jesus' twelve apostles/disciples was Simon Peter (the same man who came to Cornelius' house as mentioned earlier). After the Last Supper (the final meal that Jesus shared with his apostles/disciples in Jerusalem before his crucifixion), Jesus took the eleven disciples to the Garden of Gethsemane for prayer as he often went there with them. He told them to stay awake and pray while he went off to pray alone. As Jesus returned to them and found them sleeping, he warned Simon Peter to stay awake and pray because he knew what was coming soon. Nevertheless, he fell asleep again. By the time the soldiers had come to arrest Jesus, it was too late to pray for the strength to endure the ordeal to come. As we know Simon Peter's denial from history, he did it to Jesus three times due to weakness and fear. Yet, I certainly tell you that he did it because he hadn't been prepared himself with prayer as Jesus warned before.

Have you got my points yet? Temptation is something that we can hardly resist with our own strength but through God's word and prayer.

***

I know someone's remarkable story. He was a professional carrier man and loved drinking alcohol. He was not a believer of Jesus until he experienced a miracle in his lifetime. He became a believer of Jesus through the miracle which happened to his two-year-old toddler daughter. She got hit by a moving truck but came to life after death with his desperate prayer with a vow. He promised that he would do anything for

God if He could send his daughter's life back to him. God did it as he requested, and then he became a believer through this incident. Although he knew that God can do anything for him if he would ask, he had never asked Him to help him quit his old drinking habit. At last the time arrived for him to change. When his daughter became a seriously troubled teenager and disregarded his authority, he determined to go to the prayer meetings every Friday evening for one year. While he was praying one Friday evening like any other Friday, he heard an inner voice saying, 'Quit drinking alcohol from now on.' Drinking was his family tradition from generation to generation. So it wasn't easy for him to do so. Furthermore, he couldn't resist any offers from his colleagues after work. Here he made a deal with God saying, 'I cannot turn them down if my colleagues would offer me but I won't offer them first to go and drink after work.' A pretty cool deal! Strangely, no one offered him for drinking throughout the whole week. He was quite excited about that he hadn't had drunken almost for a week miraculously. And then he went to the Friday prayer meeting. While praying, he again heard an inner voice saying, 'Why don't you get rid of all liquor bottles at home?' He had not considered the bottles of alcohol in his home. Actually, they were gifts from his friends and guests who knew that he loved drinking. As soon as he got home after the prayer meeting, he threw out all the liquor bottles and never drank again. Is that not nice? It is the power of prayer that meant he could resist the temptation. Needless to say, his daughter is fine and now plays a great role in youth leadership at a church.

***

There is another occurrence to tell you. A mid-aged woman who is a well-known figure in public, but she was a chain smoker. She couldn't quit her old smoking habit after she became a believer of Jesus. One day she got a cigarette from a package and tried to smoke as usual. All of sudden she felt nausea and smelt something revolting. Consequently she couldn't smoke. Strangely this thing happened repeatedly whenever she tried to smoke. Finally she quit her smoking. Later on she was told that her daughter prayed for stopping her smoking. This is the power of prayer to resist temptations!

Do you have the two weapons (God's Word and prayer) to resist temptations? Not yet? Don't be discouraged. I can tell you one more thing which you can use until you will get the two weapons. Does it sound good to you?

The *Thirty-Six Stratagems* is a series of well-known war strategies which Chinese generals generally used in old times. As the name implies, there are 36 schemes to fight against the enemy. When all of 35 plans fail, then the general would choose the very last one, *the 36th scheme*. It was used when the war led to defeat, retreat and regroup. When one's side is losing, three choices remain: surrender, compromise, or escape. Surrender is complete defeat, compromise is half defeat, but escape is not defeat. As long as one is not defeated, there is still a chance to win. Thus, a Chinese saying is 'Of the Thirty-Six Stratagems, fleeing is best.' Why do I say this here? If you don't have the weapons of God's word and prayer to resist temptations yet, then I would say that 'fleeing is best.' The Bible says the same thing: avoid it, do not go to it, turn away from it, and flee from it.

Let us revisit the story of Joseph. Did I mention that he was imprisoned due to a false accusation of Potiphar's (the captain of Pharaoh's guard) wife? Actually, she liked young and good looking Joseph and attempted to seduce him on several occasions. When he refused her sexual temptation, he ran off, leaving his garment (*kalasiris*; ancient Egyptian clothing) in her hands. So she retaliated by falsely accusing him of trying to rape her. When Potiphar was told her made-up story, he flew into a rage and had Joseph imprisoned. Although he was imprisoned, he did not fall into the temptation by fleeing indeed. Do you think that Joseph was silly to choose the 'fleeing and imprisonment' option as opposed to the option of 'sleeping with her and getting promoted'? Well, if he would choose the latter, could it be possible for him to be the second-in-command in Egypt later? Actually, he met pharaoh's chief cupbearer and chief baker in the dungeon of Potiphar where he was imprisoned. One night both of them had dreamed, and he interpreted the dreams for them. As he interpreted, the baker was hanged whereas the cupbearer was restored to his position three days later on Pharaoh's birthday. When Pharaoh had dreams two years later, then the chief cupbearer brought to his attention a young Hebrew slave whom he met in that dungeon. Joseph was called in and interpreted Pharaoh's dreams and became the second-in-command in Egypt afterwards. What a great choice he made! Aha! Fleeing from the temptation really worked with him, didn't it?

***

Friend, if you are struggling with particular temptations and found it difficult to resist them, you can pray with me now. Please pray it aloud from your heart and truly believe it. Lift up your hands as a gesture of your surrender if desired. Or kneel down if it works better for you. Anyway pray it sincerely and ask the Spirit of God (Holy Spirit) to help you. Also, please pray with an expectation that the supernatural power of God will come upon you as you pray.

Father in Heaven,
I'm sorry for what I have done wrong so far.
Now I ask you to forgive me for all my sins.

When _____ (your bad habit(s)) tempts me,
please help me not to fall into it.
Please fill me with your Spirit.
I pray this in Jesus' name.
Amen.

Congratulations, Friend! You made it. Whenever the temptation comes along, please remember this prayer and pray to God for a help. Trust Him always. He will never fail you.

♥ Pause and Write Your Thoughts So Far

Eight

But Deliver Us From The Evil One

Have you ever been in a situation where you could not get over it all by yourself? You looked hopeless. There seemed to be no one who was around you to help you out. Try to recall how you passed through that time and then moved forward. I am sure that you have your own story to tell me about it. Here I would like to share more stories with you: some are others' whereas some are mine. When we read and watch news, some people's stories are remarkable when they tell us how they survived and were rescued and delivered. Some were in trouble due to their own faults whereas some were in danger due to other's wickedness. No matter what caused them to get in trouble, it is good to hear how they survived and were saved at the end.

A few people in the Bible had gone through tough times and tell us their dramatic, amazing, and exciting stories. One of them is Daniel (meaning 'God is my judge') or Belteshazzar (meaning 'Bel's prince'; Bel was the principal god of Babylon). In his teens, he and others were taken captive to Babylon because the Babylonian king Nebuchadnezzar destroyed the kingdom of Judah, and its capital, Jerusalem in 586 BC. Although he had to leave his home country and live in a foreign land, he did not leave his faith on God. Furthermore, God gave him an excellent spirit and ability to study. After all of his training was done, he was promoted to a high rank of government. When the time of trials came to him, he had made up his mind and stood firm and didn't compromise on his faith.

One of the hardest trials he faced was whether he would give up his prayers to God which he usually did three times every day when the Babylonian king prohibited praying to any other gods except him for 30 days. The punishment for anyone who disobeyed this edict was to be thrown to the lions. Nevertheless, Daniel solemnly continued to pray before God. As a result, he was arrested and put in a den of hungry lions. A huge stone was rolled over the entrance and sealed by the king's signet ring. There was neither an exit nor other means of protection. Now you can imagine that he was in a dark den surrounded by roaring and hungry lions. What would you do if you were in that den at that time? Was he scared to death? I assume that he was praying although I don't know what he did exactly at the time. Then an absolutely remarkable thing happened at night. The light shone bright in the darkness, and an angel sent by God shut the mouths of the lions. The hungry lions became calm like tamed cats in front of his eyes. In awe he praised and thanked God who rescued him from the lion's mouths throughout the night. Needless to say, he was rescued from the den in the following morning when the king had realised that Daniel's God saved him from the lions.

***

There is another Jewish man called Jonah from Gath-hepher of the northern kingdom of Israel in 772-754 BC. God picked Jonah and told him to go to Nineveh (the capital of the powerful ancient Assyrian empire, located in modern-day northern Iraq) and warn the wicked people of Nineveh that if they didn't repent, they would be destroyed within 40 days. God is merciful and wanted to show compassion to the people of Nineveh and gave them an opportunity to turn from evil and to serve the one who created and loved them. Yet, Jonah didn't want to go to that wicked place. Did you ask me why? I assume that he thought that the Assyrians were wicked enemies and deserved to be destroyed. So he got on a boat that was sailing west to Tarshish (Spain in the modern day). In fact, Tarshish stood more than 2,500 miles from Israel in the opposite direction of Nineveh.

While Jonah was on board, God hurled a great wind and storm, and the ship was ready to sink. He was sleeping, and the captain yelled at him to call out to his God to rescue them from the storm. He had told the crew that he was running from God and his errand. Hence, Jonah was thrown into the sea. Immediately, the storm stopped, and God commanded a huge fish to swallow Jonah. There he stayed in the belly of that fish for three days and nights. Think about being wet, cold, and afraid in the dark! The lion's den for Daniel was terrifying. How about being in the belly of a fish? Perhaps seaweed was wrapped around his head, and he was floating in water nearly drowning. He had nothing to do but cry out to God. Then he came to his mind that God is the only answer - He is the one who can rescue and save him! Of course, he cried from the belly of the fish. God told the fish to throw him up. Jonah was rescued at the end and carried out his errand afterwards.

***

Near the Sea of Galilee in Israel is the city of Decapolis in Gerasenes. There lived a man who was filled with unclean spirits. In modern days, he could be in a mental hospital. He no longer lived at home but in the graveyard. I don't know how long he lived like that. Poor man! Neither chains nor shackles were strong enough to restrain him or keep him locked up for his own safety and the safety of others. He would cut himself with stones, and he would cry and scream in the graveyard and on the mountainside day and night. Everyone in the town tried to avoid him and was very scared of him.

One day Jesus came to town by boat on the Sea of Galilee. As he got out of the boat, this crazy man saw Jesus and ran and bowed before him. He pleaded with Jesus to leave him alone, even calling him the son of the most High God. As Jesus compassionately looked him in the eye and calmly asked him his name. The man replied that it was 'Legion' because so many unclean spirits dwelt in him. Then Jesus commanded the evil spirits to leave the man. They had to obey, and their new dwelling place was a herd of about 2,000 pigs which stampeded down a steep bank into the Sea of Galilee. The herdsmen ran scared to the town to let everyone know what had happened.

Then the people came to see for themselves, and they found the man sitting at the feet of Jesus, dressed and in his right mind! Fear spread because they knew that for years they had watched him hurt and destroy himself and frighten anyone who dared come near. They asked Jesus to leave since they could not make sense of what had happened. So, Jesus got into the boat but told this transformed man to stay and give witness to what great things his rescuer had done for him. God is so good!

***

Now I would like to tell you my own story that happened a long time ago. In my early twenties I loved travelling alone and visited many countries in Europe, Asia, and America and enjoyed their culture as well as local food. During my school holiday my Swiss friend invited me to join her commissioning service for her missionary work. I was pleased to accept her suggestion and went to Switzerland during the Easter break. A schoolmate knew that I was in Switzerland around that time and asked me to stop by her place which is a different part of the nation. (Actually, I still don't remember the names of her place and of the street where my friend's house was.) With my friend's help, I went to my schoolmate's place and was supposedly to be back by the time when the service began.

After meeting with my schoolmate, I said to her that I needed to leave her place to get back in time. She asked me where I was supposed to go. I showed her my friend's home address. She said that she knew the place and was not far from her place. I thought that it was strange because it took me some time to get to her place. Anyway, we both left her place, and my schoolmate told the ticket office where I was supposed to go and got a ticket for me. I got on board, and then when I got off the train stop as shown in the ticket, I noticed that it was a totally strange place. I walked around a bit and tried to ask people where I was. Unfortunately, nobody was able to speak English. So I went back to the train station and asked the ticket officer where I was and showed him my friend's address. I was told that I got a wrong train and needed to go to Zurich where I could catch another train to go to my friend's house. What a shock! I ended up in a strange place with a misspelled name of the place. A panic came over me, and then I was so worried to get to my friend's place in time. I just managed to get on a train heading to Zurich. There was no one in that coach where I got in. I sat down and closed my eyes and urgently prayed in tears, 'Father in Heaven, please help me. I don't know whether I can go back to my friend's house since I cannot find anyone who can speak English now. I'm already late to be in the service. Furthermore, her parents cannot speak English, and I don't speak German, either. So I have no idea how to tell them about what happened to me since my friend won't be home. Help me!'

After this prayer, I opened my eyes and saw a lady in a red winter coat who sat next to me. She started to talk to me in English fluently. Without thinking too much, I told her everything that I had gone through. Strangely enough, she absolutely understood what I murmured in tears and encouraged me with her experiences in the past. She also had a terrible experience with air travel. She ended up with a totally different nation due to a spelling error. In that sense, I was fortunate because I was still in the same country. Also, she willingly would make a call on my behalf and tell my friend's parents to pick me up from the place where I would arrive. When we got to Zurich, she took me to the place where I should take a train and phoned my friend's home. As the train arrived, she said goodbye to me and took an escalator and disappeared from my eyes. Was she an angel to rescue me at that time? I don't know whether she was an angel or not. Seemingly, she was an angel to me at that time.

***

I don't say that all of us fall into the evil's hand due to our shortcomings. It is similar to going into a coal mine where you can get dirt or you would breathe unclean air if you get exposed to air pollution, and so on and so forth. We might be able to avoid and flee from certain places and moments which could lead us into temptations. What does the Bible say about it? Flee from temptation and resist it with the word of God. If you fail, then repent quickly and ask God for deliverance. If you are in trouble now, please pray with me.

Father in Heaven,
I'm sorry that I failed you.
Please forgive me for my sin.
Now deliver me from this trouble.
Thank you for being here for me.
I pray this in Jesus' name.
Amen.

♥ **Pause and Write Your Thoughts So Far**

EPILOGUE

You have come along with me so far without failure. I don't think that you got this book by chance and read it regardless of the fact that you have enjoyed it or not. In the beginning of the book, I shared my daydreaming experience. Let us think about it for a moment and ruminate on 'why you are here on the earth and especially now.' In fact, this ultimate question compelled me to write the book because many people don't seem to know the answer for that question. Perhaps you might have an answer before or after reading the book, then I would like to encourage you. Press on and keep up the good work! It is worthy no matter what! Even you can encourage others to read the book. All of us are here once and then will be gone some day. If we would know the reason that we live for, then our life would be totally different from 'what we are now.'

Whether you have noticed it or not, I have titled each chapter from the well-known prayer which Jesus taught his disciples as he was asked to teach them to pray. There are subtle differences among English Bible versions in terms of translation. Yet, I believe that the core ingredients are the same as below:

Our Father in Heaven
Your name must be holy
Your kingdom come

Your will be done here as it is in Heaven
Give us today our daily needs
Forgive our sins as we forgive those who sin against us
Do not let us yield to temptation
But deliver us from the evil one
[For yours is the kingdom, the power and the glory forever].

The prayer above is found in the Bible, especially the books of Matthew and Luke (the first two books in the New Testament of the Bible). Any Western Christian who is not an adherent of the Catholic Church or Eastern Orthodox Church is called 'Protestant Christians.' They do pray this with one more sentence added in brackets. *It is called the doxology* (a short praise to God) which possibly was added by the early Christians (of the early fifth or late fourth century). Whether or not this doxology was, in fact, added in some manuscripts versus omitted in others is debatable. One thing for sure is that ancient Jews regularly added or used doxologies to conclude their prayers. So you can pray this prayer every day with the doxology. I said 'everyday'! You cannot pray 'Give us today our daily needs' if it isn't our daily prayer, can you?

Father God has a special plan for you which only you can do. I do usually illustrate it in this way. He has created a big masterpiece of jigsaw puzzles which everyone has a piece to fit into it. Some pieces are colourful with more pictures as opposed to some with simple black or white. We shouldn't compare ours with others because we don't know what the whole picture in that masterpiece looks like. In this respect, all pieces are equally important and unique in shape and colour so that others cannot fit into the place where yours is exactly supposed to be. The masterpiece won't be nice at all if you haven't done your part. Imagine the nearly complete jigsaw puzzles' picture with one missing piece! The important point is not 'what jigsaw piece (you have) looks like' but 'how well you fit into the whole picture with yours.' I hope it makes sense to you.

***

Now you are ready to go for your life mission on the earth, aren't you? For the first practical step, I have prepared a 30 days' diary of your journey with God below. **Everyday** pray the prayer that Jesus taught and try to listen to God while waiting quietly. Then write down whatever He tells you and whatever He asks you to do for the day. Perhaps you can pray something like this: 'Father in Heaven, please tell me what is in your heart today.'; 'Father in Heaven, please tell me whom you want me to bless today.'; 'Father in Heaven, please teach me how to honour You today.' and so on and so forth. If you are not well disciplined to do this every day, you can find your accountability person who can help you out for 30 days (and even more). I pray that your life will be totally different 30 days later.

Okay! Now it's time to say goodbye to you. I wish you the very best and pray for successful completing of your life mission on the earth.

Finally, to the one (like you) who is ready to go for a journey with God from now and onwards,

The Lord bless you and keep you;
The Lord make His face to shine upon you,
and be gracious to you;
The Lord lift His countenance upon you,
and give you peace.

My Journey With God

S	M	T	W	T	F	S
					1	2
3	4	5	6	7	8	9
10	11	12	13	14	15	16
17	18	19	20	21	22	23
24	25	26	27	28	29	30

DAY 1

DAY 2

DAY 3

DAY 4

DAY 5

DAY 6

DAY 7

DAY 8

DAY 9

DAY 10

DAY 11

DAY 12

DAY 13

DAY 14

DAY 15

DAY 16

DAY 17

DAY 18

DAY 19

DAY 20

DAY 21

DAY 22

DAY 23

DAY 24

DAY 25

DAY 26

DAY 27

DAY 28

DAY 29

DAY 30

N.B.

- ➢ When the 30 days' journey with God is over, please don't stop here but continue to keep your journaling.

- ➢ At the end of each chapter I have spared a page for **Pause and Write Your Thoughts So Far** to jot down your thoughts while reading. I have thought that it would give you time to think more in depth before moving to the next chapter. I believe that it is helpful to spend more time to reflect on that topic and to pour out your thoughts and feelings. *Writing* as a visualisation technique definitely helps you manifest something in your mind.

- ➢ My another book, *Shofar-Blowing: Sounds From Heaven To Earth* is highly recommend for your spiritual pursuit.

Author's Note

I grabbed my computer to write this book with a strong desire. Actually it was triggered from the moment when I had an encounter with a gentleman called, John.

One afternoon I was walking on the river bank as usual. John had noticed that I was a newcomer in Spalding, Lincolnshire. He did dog walking three times everyday but hadn't seen me before. Certainly it was a coincidental meeting I would say! We talked about many things while walking with his old dog since she was very slow to follow us. At the end of our conversation, I asked him whether he believes in God. He did say neither 'yes' nor 'no' but paused and kept silent for a while. At the moment I wished that I had more time to talk about what he needs to know about 'life after death' but had to go to the different direction from the way where he was heading off.

Every day I see people pass by and die without knowing where they are going after death. It is a fundamental matter that we need to make a serious decision before our time runs out here on the earth. Sadly, many miss the opportunity to know about it because they either have never heard of or known about the truth of the life after death and because they were born and grown up in surrounding circumstances that were impossible to pursue the truth.

About The Author

Hana has lived in various countries and was involved in missions in the past. She has a husband and a 13 year-old daughter. She studied in a wide range of academic disciplines in Pharmacy, Healing Ministry, Christian Counselling, Anthropology, Missiology, English Language Teaching, and Linguistics. Hana and her family participated in *Celebration for the Nations* in Wales (2007-2014 and 2016-2017), and founded and ran *Celebration Colchester* for two years until they went to Mozambique to be part of 'Harvest School'(*Iris Global*) in June-October, 2015. She and her husband are the co-founders of *Nehemiah 9.3 Mission* (www.nehemiah93.com)

Lightning Source UK Ltd.
Milton Keynes UK
UKHW010735040921
389992UK00001B/60

9 781399 902236